PLANNING YOUR PERFECT

Wedding

Written by
Janet & Philip Raby

PLANNING YOUR PERFECT
Wedding

This edition first published in the UK in 2006
by Green Umbrella

www.greenumbrella.co.uk

© Green Umbrella Publishing 2006

Publishers Jules Gammond, Tim Exell,
Vanessa Gardner

Printed and bound in China

ISBN 1-905009-35-6

Contents

So you're going to get married

OK, let's make an assumption. You've just decided to get married and you're at the early stages of planning it. You may just have got engaged in the last few days, and you're on a high, excited about the big day ahead, and keen to read anything you can about weddings.

Well, congratulations. Making a commitment to spend the rest of your life with someone is great news (and, that's what getting married is all about.) and not something to take on lightly. But we're not here to spout on about your long-term future; you'll be getting enough of that from your family, future in-laws, friends, vicar and postman. No, the sole purpose of this book is to make sure that your married life kicks off just the way you want it to. In other words, to make sure you have a fantastic wedding.

BELOW Getting engaged is exciting, and you have lots of plans to make over the coming months – enjoy it!

Planning makes perfect

There are three words you need to keep in mind to ensure a perfect wedding – planning, planning and planning. Plan the day carefully and properly and you'll minimise the risk of things going wrong. That's not to say nothing will go wrong – things will – but you should avoid any major problems.

If you fail to plan, you plan to fail. OK, so it's the sort of thing your future father-in-law would (and undoubtedly will) say, but avoid this advice at your peril, or you could end up with a day to remember, but not in the way you'd hoped.

"We fixed a date for our wedding and told our families," recalls Cathy. "But when we contacted the vicar the church was already booked and so we had to change the date. Then once that was all finalised we couldn't get a venue for the reception – everywhere seemed to be booked up at least a year in advance. We ended up putting off the whole thing for a year."

So if you're thinking of having a big wedding in a few months' time, think again. You need to book reception venues and, very often, churches at least a year in advance, sometimes as much as two years ahead, for the more popular places.

Money matters

However, before you start booking anything, you need to have some idea of what sort of wedding you want, and that depends largely on money. The average wedding in the UK costs £15,000 today. You need to decide now what you can afford – it may be more or less than the average, but whatever your budget is, you have to stick to it.

BELOW Spend time with each other, deciding what you want from the big day

That, though, is easier said than done, as Andy and Gemma found out. "We set a budget of £12,000 and that sounded plenty," recalls Andy, who's an accountant and should know better. "However, the guest list grew and grew as we had to accommodate various friends and distant relatives whom we couldn't offend. And then we wanted a band, and the cake cost a fortune, too. We ended up spending over £16,000 and are still paying it off three years later. Still it was a good day!"

So how do you decide on a budget? It depends on who's going to pay for the day. Traditionally, the bride's father (remember, women didn't get involved in money in the good old days) footed the bill for pretty much everything. All the groom had to fork out for was suits for him and his best man and ushers, flowers and church fees. Oh, and the bride was expected to pay for her haircut and make-up.

Stressful day

BELOW Get it right, and your wedding day will be fun

You're probably thinking that this sounds like a good deal (especially for the bride) and most of the time it is, but be warned that some brides' mothers assume that because their husbands are signing the cheques, they can have full control of the event. "We wanted a quiet, informal wedding," recalls Gail. "However, my mum got involved and, because her and dad were paying, we couldn't really argue when they

started planning a massive do with loads of guests we didn't know. Even the jazz band we ended up with was not what we wanted. The whole thing was very stressful and we don't have happy memories of the day at all."

This is one reason that these days the couple often choose to foot the bill themselves, sometimes taking out a loan to do so. Often, the parents on both sides will make a contribution, perhaps in lieu of a wedding present. If you're going to look after the finances yourself, it's a good idea to set up a separate 'wedding' bank account, so you can start saving up right from the start, and will be able to keep track of where the money's going (and it will start going very quickly!).

And while on the subject, wedding insurance is a good idea. It will cover things such as damage or loss of the wedding dress, presents, problems with the venue (bookings have been known to be lost) and cancellation due to serious illness (no, that doesn't include a bad hangover from the night before!) or death of a close family member. Insurance won't pay out if the bride or groom gets jilted, but it may cover the cost of counselling!

BELOW You two are the most important people at your wedding

Set a budget

Whoever is paying the bills, it's not difficult to work out a budget. And then you need to cut your cloth to suit. If money is tight, you can't have 400 guests sitting down to a four-course meal on a private island with Elton John tinkling the ivories in the background. Don't despair, though, 30 people tucking into a buffet at the local village hall with a CD player in the corner can make for just as memorable a day.

But only if it's planned properly, and for that to happen, someone needs to take charge. Who that is needs to be decided fairly early on and the decision made clear to everyone else involved. The modern solution is for the bride and groom to work together to plan the day, but that's not always possible. One partner could be away working a lot or may not be interested, or if the parents are paying for the wedding they may want to have a say in the proceedings. Just make sure that someone has the final say.

Make a date

One thing you do both need to liaise on, though, is the actual date of the wedding. It's all very well setting an arbitrary day (usually a Saturday for the convenience of guests) a year or more in the future, but do check it doesn't clash with anything else. For instance, you could end up picking the same date as your parents' silver wedding (which may or may not cause a problem), or a major sporting event; something which is bound to cause grief. "We chose our wedding date because it was the only Saturday the hotel was free," recalls

BELOW Your wedding should be the happiest day of your life

Jane. "As the big day loomed we found out why. The FA Cup final was on that date, and some of the guests were not happy. In fact, as soon as we got to the reception, half the wedding party disappeared into the bar to watch the footy on television. Thankfully, my new husband isn't into football, so he remained on-hand!"

Oh, and just to digress onto a delicate subject for a moment. Girls – do think about what time of the month the wedding is going to be. You do want to be able to make the most of that bridal suite, don't you?

What do you want?

One thing that you two should decide for yourselves is what you both want from the day (and we'll assume it's not a game of football). Are you after a fairytale wedding, a great party with all your mates, a family reunion, or a romantic day for two? You're going to have pressure from relatives to do something you don't want, especially if someone else is paying, but stick to your guns. Of course, you may have to compromise – a bungee jumping wedding in New Zealand could upset elderly parents who don't feel they can make the trip (not to mention the jump), while a full-blown Latin Mass may concern your

staunch Protestant future in-laws. Whatever you decide, though, make sure that, first and foremost, it's going to be a wedding that you will both enjoy and remember for many years to come.

Who's involved?

Early on in the proceedings, you'll want to think about who's going to be involved in the wedding. It's usual to include both sets of parents, but you'll also want a best man. Usually this is a brother or close friend of the groom, and should be someone you both like and trust. Traditionally, the best man takes charge of the ushers and the groom, making sure they're all dressed properly with the appropriate button-holes, and holds the rings (the subject of many a comedy sketch). These days, though, his role is more casual – he drives the groom to the wedding, stands next to him, hands over the rings at the appropriate juncture and then makes a highly amusing and often embarrassing speech at the reception. And that's something you

BELOW The Best Man should be someone close to the Groom

BELOW You can have as few or as many bridesmaids as you like

OPPOSITE Children are very cute as bridesmaids

should bear in mind when you choose a best man. Make sure he's someone you can trust not to embarrass you in front of family and friends. "I didn't know our best man very well," remembers Laura, "but my fiancé insisted he was a great mate and just the man for the job. However, he had too much to drink at the reception and by the time he made his speech he could hardly stand up. He made rude remarks about our sex life and had me and my mother in tears. Needless to say, we've not had anything to do with him since then."

Bridesmaids

Still, at least he didn't get off with a bridesmaid, which is another tradition for the best man to do. And bridesmaids are, traditionally, the bride's equivalent of the best man, only she can have more than one if she wants. Although before you choose a team of 12 cute little girls bear in mind that each will have to have a dress and accessories, which will have an impact on your budget.

Also, although very young bridesmaids may look cute for a while, but they can often get tired and hungry and may not always perform on cue. "I wanted my two nieces as bridesmaids," smiles Becky. "The eldest was eight and she was lovely, but her three-year-old sister called out in a loud voice bang in the middle of the service that she needed a poo! It was very funny but did detract from the solemness of the ceremony."

BELOW Who can resist a little girl as a bridesmaid?

OPPOSITE Plan it carefully, and your wedding will be like a fairytale

An adult bridesmaid (or matron of honour if they're married) is less likely to be incontinent and will have the added benefit of being able to help the bride get ready and give her much needed moral support while she's rushing around getting her hair and make-up done. Just make sure she doesn't get off with that best man!

Ushering in

The other key players in a traditional wedding are the ushers. Basically, they greet the guests as they arrive, hand them an order of service and direct them to their seats. Traditionally, they also support the best man throughout the day and help ensure that the guests know where they're going and when. You should have at least two ushers and, ideally, they should be people you can rely on. In reality, though, you tend to ask the friends who you want to placate for not being given the best man's job!

So, in a nutshell, that's the start of your wedding plans. Lots to think about, and now it's time to go into a bit more detail. Remember – planning is everything.

The venue

A fter deciding to get married, deciding on the venue(s) is the next most important thing to consider and that's where the planning process really begins. In life, whatever the occasion, the venue is of paramount importance and this goes for weddings as much as anything else.

Depending on the type of wedding you want, you may need to decide on two venues – one for the ceremony and a second for the reception – or in the case of a civil wedding you could stay at one place for the whole day.

BELOW A church is a traditional venue for UK weddings

Whatever you decide, the environment in which you choose to tie the knot and celebrate will go a long way to setting the tone for the day, as David testifies. "We chose to get married in Romsey Abbey, where my family always went to church. It's a fabulous old building but, unfortunately, rather too large and our modest group of fifty guests seemed lost in it. Looking back, a smaller church would have been more intimate, but at least it was somewhere that meant something to us."

Julie had a rather different experience. "We were married in a local registry office, because we're not religious. The problem was, it was on a main road in a not very nice part of town, and my new husband and I walked out onto a narrow pavement with lots of cars and lorries driving past. Not very romantic!"

The ceremony venue

People usually get married in a church, chapel or registry office, right? Well, yes they do but there's a lot more choice than that when it comes to choosing a venue. Think about it; we live in a multi-cultural society that has embraced so many different religions and ways of life that there's no such thing as 'normal' any more. And religion does still exert an enormous influence on the lives of billions of people, with a wedding ceremony being, not only the celebration of the love two people have for each other, but a celebration of one's faith and traditions.

So, if you're religious then you're likely to marry in the place that you or your family uses for worship. If you're Jewish it'll be a synagogue, if you're Jehovah's Witnesses it'll be a Kingdom Hall, if you're Muslim it'll be a mosque and if you're both atheists it'll probably be a hotel or registry office! We're sure you get the picture but religion and weddings are inextricably linked and that goes for anywhere in the world, not just the UK.

Problems when choosing a mutually agreeable venue often arise when people of two differing faiths are getting married and often it's best to use a 'neutral' venue such as a registry office when this is the case. However, family pressures over this matter can be unbelievably strong and it's best to start out as you mean to go on. As a couple you've obviously discussed a great many things that will impact on your life together, far outweighing anything that the actual wedding day may bring and any difference in faith will have been considered during the first few weeks of a serious relationship. After all, almost every war that has been fought in history can have its roots traced back to a difference in religious belief. Ignore this one at your peril because things get even more complicated once children enter the picture...

OPPOSITE A modern registry office can be as romantic as a church

BELOW Different faiths have their own variations on the wedding service

"I'm Catholic and my wife is Protestant" explains Michael. "Because she's from Northern Ireland, there was a problem knowing where to get married, even though I get on well with her family. In the end, we decided to get married in a registry office and then, on separate days, we were blessed in our own churches."

The venue chosen for the actual ceremony is nowhere near as important as the actual vows you'll be making so try to keep things in perspective and don't allow things to become fractious or bitter at such an early stage in preparations – this is supposed to be fun!

Home and away

ABOVE Choose a venue that suits the number of guests

It's the most romantic thing in the world when two people prove their love for one another by getting married, so it's only natural that many couples prefer to say 'I do' in surroundings more conducive to romance than rainswept Britain. What could be more lovely than a paradise wedding in Hawaii, the Seychelles, the Caribbean or Sri Lanka?

"When Max and I were married in Hawaii it was simply perfect," gushes Helen. "He used to live out there for months at a time so knew the right places. It was intimate and incredibly emotional and we recited our vows on a beach in the middle of nowhere and in the presence of a handful of our closest friends and relatives. We had garlands of fresh flowers around our necks and the photographs will be treasured by us for the rest of our lives." Sounds wonderful, doesn't it?

Max and Helen didn't want the friends and colleagues that weren't able to make it to the Hawaiian ceremony to miss out, so they had their marriage blessed a couple of weeks after returning home from honeymoon. This took place at a beautiful church in their village, followed by a reception at a nearby hotel and it enabled everyone to share in their big day without the need to travel to the other side of the planet. "It was like getting married twice without the divorce," says Helen.

Yes, a tropical wedding is a dream for many but isn't out of reach for most of us? Well, long-haul travel specialist Kuoni reckons not: "The average cost of a Kuoni wedding overseas," the company claims, "including an exotic honeymoon for two, is less than £3000. A fraction of the price of marrying in the UK and a fraction of the hassle." If this is true they do have a point...

BELOW Getting married abroad has its attractions

PLANNING YOUR PERFECT *Wedding* 23

RIGHT A beachside
wedding is many
people's dream

RIGHT A beachside wedding is many people's dream

As with almost anything in life, there are pros and cons whichever way you choose to get married. A tropical wedding could seem like a good idea but you'll have less control over the day's activities and many people on your ideal guest list may not be able to attend for one reason or another. Then there's the weather: If you think Wales is wet then just consider that the tropics have seemingly endless months of constant rain (though, to be fair, it's usually still warm) and the conditions can get pretty extreme, especially in certain months – usually, it has to be said, the cheapest months.

One thing the tropical wedding offers, as a distinct advantage, is the combined wedding and honeymoon destination. This is where Kuoni's sales patter starts to make sense because you'll already be there, reducing the costs of your honeymoon by combining it within the whole 'package'. There are, of course, plenty of horror stories associated with overseas weddings if you look for them – anything from the bride and groom feeling as though they're on a conveyor belt awaiting their turn while the favoured local girl is treated like royalty, to hotels being infested with cockroaches and mosquitoes. British brides and grooms have been through it all and often continue to accept second best when it comes to the big day with tearful and angry guests (usually wedding invitees) that can't cope with anything that's out of the ordinary. Remember that wherever in the world it happens to take place, it's actually your day.

"We got married in Sri Lanka," recalls Emma. "We thought it was lovely with wonderful people and scenery, but my parents, who'd never travelled further than Tenerife, hated it, and moaned about the food, the heat and the locals. I wish we hadn't invited them!"

If an overseas wedding isn't for you but you'd still like to do something a little different, how about getting married in Scotland? Gretna Green is a favourite destination for many because of its history. It all began in 1753 when the English Parliament passed an act which said that, unless both parties getting married were at least 21 years old, then consent had to be given by the parents.

In Scotland, however, this law did not apply and, if they really wanted to, boys could marry at 14 and girls at 12 without their parents' consent. So it made sense for English

BELOW Marrying abroad can be an opportunity for your friends and family to have a holiday!

sweethearts to elope to Scotland to tie the knot against the parents' wishes.

And it just so happened that the first and easiest place for these rebellious youngsters to get to was Gretna Green, just over the border in Dumfries and Galloway. Until the mid-19th Century many weddings were performed in the Old Blacksmith's Shop but then a Scottish law was passed that stated that you had to be a resident of Scotland to get married in the country.

Today, though, English couples can once again get married in Greta Green, and it's become a popular venue. Not for sweethearts escaping bullying parents, though, but rather for couples attracted by the romance and history of the place. Indeed, after an official ceremony at the registry office, you can have your photographs taken in the Old Blacksmith's Shop and think of all the couples who have done the same over the years.

Of course, the locals have made the most of Gretna's appeal and the town is full of companies offering everything you'll need for your wedding, and you don't even have to visit the place in advance to organise it. Do a search on the Internet and you'll find lots of people vying for your business.

And now for something completely different

Bungee jumping, sky diving, scuba diving, rollercoaster riding, dressing up as Elvis: you name it and it's been done when it comes to getting married. If you think of a novel way of getting married, chances are it's been done before. About the only thing yet to happen is a marriage conducted in outer space – but it's bound to happen one day.

Do think carefully about doing anything too wacky, though – what's fun for you may not suit your extended family. Can you see your granny on a rollercoaster? And what is the relevance of the idea? If you're both keen scuba divers, for instance, then an underwater wedding could mean a lot to you both, but doing it 'just to be different' isn't necessarily a good enough reason.

OPPOSITE An old ship offers a unique backdrop to your wedding

BELOW Some venues let you have the wedding and reception under one roof

And if you do choose an unusual wedding, it's a good idea to follow it with a more conventional reception that all your guests – young and old – can enjoy. Oh, and please don't ask your guests to dress up in wet-suits or Elvis wigs just because you are – they won't appreciate it!

All under one roof

The venue for the reception is covered in Chapter eight, but bear in mind that, these days, you can have a civil wedding anywhere that has the necessary license – you're not just limited to a church or registry office.

This is good news for non-religious couples, because it gives you much more scope than a registry office which, in some cases, isn't the most attractive place. The usual choice is a hotel and more and more are geared up to perform weddings. Good hotels will liaise with the registrar on your behalf, to ensure that someone will be there to perform the service on the day.

When choosing a hotel, think about what you need. There has to be a room large enough to accommodate all the guests during the ceremony with comfortable seating that gives everyone a view of the proceedings. It's preferable for this to be a pleasant and private room, away from other guests.

And what about photographs? Does the hotel have attractive grounds where you and the photographer can go to for some lovely shots?

Then you'll need to ensure the hotel can cope with the sort of reception you want. Does it produce the sort of food you like? Is there enough room for a disco? What time will the evening have to draw to a close?

So, although there are real advantages in holding the entire day under one roof, there are more demands on the venue if you don't want to compromise.

Your guests and you

These days, it's usual for some wedding guests to have to travel long distances to attend the ceremony – sometimes even from overseas. So it's a good idea to ensure that they can stay in the hotel where the wedding is taking place. Bear in mind, though, that not all your guests will be able to afford a luxury hotel room, so you may need to find cheaper Bed and Breakfast-type accommodation nearby.

Make a list of accommodation in the area and send it to anyone who asks, and be willing to help your guests find somewhere to stay – they're going out of their way to be with you on your big day, so the least you can do is make it as easy as possible for them.

And don't forget yourselves – make sure you book the bridal suite, if there is one, or at least the best room in the hotel, well in advance. You don't want to end up being in two single beds on your wedding night, do you?

Here comes the bride

There's no getting away from the fact that when it comes to the big day, all eyes are on the bride and what she dares to wear. There are hundreds of different styles of gowns available these days but when it comes to first marriages, many women simply can't shake off their childhood fantasy of looking like a fairy-tale princess, so they choose a reasonably traditional wedding dress with all the trimmings.

Others, particularly those opting for a civil wedding, may prefer to buy an outfit which is somewhat less showy and a little more 'streamlined'.

And, of course, if you're going for a parachute jump or underwater wedding, then you may have to be a little more creative with your choice of outfit.

If you're getting married for the second time it is entirely up to you whether you choose a bridal gown or go for something such as a smart, sophisticated suit.

Hiring a dress can be an option or you could be lucky enough to snap up a second-hand one which looks as good as new. Let's face it, the chances are it will have had little wear and tear. Scour the classified department in the local newspaper for bargain buys, or visit a shop that specialises in pre-owned bridal wear.

BELOW A traditional white dress has a timeless appeal

Whatever your decision, it's worth taking plenty of time to choose the outfit you feel most comfortable in; one that suits not just your figure but also reflects your own personality.

Remember, those wedding photographs will probably take pride of place in your home for many years to come. Don't wear something that will haunt you forever with thoughts of 'if only I'd gone for something different'.

Making that choice

Although it's important to get your image right, picking the gown of your dreams should be great fun – one of the best 'dressing up' sessions you will have experienced since childhood!

Jackie recalls: "To make the choosing easier, I took along my best friend. I knew she'd give me both moral support and an honest opinion to ensure I didn't impulse buy and then regret my decision as the wedding got nearer.

"We visited several shops and had a ball trying on all the different styles. In the end I decided to forget the off-the-peg dresses and went to a rather upmarket bridal specialist who created my dream dress. It did cost a little bit more but, in the great scheme of things, I felt it was well worth the money.

"I had regular fittings right up to a few days before the wedding to make sure the dress was perfect. When I arrived at the church I really felt that I looked fantastic. Even my own sister was surprised at how the whole outfit had come together. I have to admit that I just felt like a million dollars all day!"

Do try to stick to your budget. It is easy to get carried away but if you walk into a shop with a fixed price in mind it should help.

Think about the season. Winter weddings can be fabulous but do dress appropriately. If you're having photographs taken outside there's no point in being uncomfortably cold. Consider some sort of cloak or stole to keep hypothermia at bay!

Seek out the professionals

Browsing wedding magazines is a great way of discovering the type of dress that

OPPOSITE A splash of colour and some delicate embroidery adds a dash of vintage charm

BELOW Winter dresses have a charm of their own

BELOW With careful attention to detail you're bound to feel like a princess on your wedding day

takes your fancy. Once you have some idea of the kind of look you're after, it is important to seek advice from the professionals and try on different styles. Established bridal specialists will be able to recommend dresses to accentuate your good points and detract from any others.

Don't forget that guests will be admiring your outfit from both the front and the back, so pay plenty of attention to how you look from all angles.

Remember all the practicalities, even if it seems like a fairly insignificant detail. For instance, if you're having a church wedding and feel

a long train is for you, remember to think about finding some way of hooking it up if you aim to dance the night away at the reception.

BELOW Remember that people are going to be seeing the back of you for much of the service

Specialist advice

Helen Coster of Confetti & Lace in Farnham regularly offers women advice on choosing their dream gown in her capacity as shop manager. "Strapless is one of the most popular styles at the moment. Many brides-to-be are going for soft A-line shapes with a little bit of detail. Lace-up backs are also extremely in," she says. "One of our biggest sellers is a designer called Maggie Sottero who designs dresses that seem to fit particularly well and give brides a lot of design quality for their money."

When it comes to colour, these days most brides shun white in favour of the more subtle hues of ivory or diamond white. Helen adds: "White just isn't popular at all. I don't think it suits a lot of skin tones and can look quite harsh. Ivory or diamond-white is certainly more forgiving."

For those more daring brides, bold-coloured dresses can look stunning. However, if you do go for a bright shade, it may be a good idea to keep the detail to a minimum. "Wine red has been very trendy lately and light gold is also becoming more popular, Helen continues.

"I think lilac is going to be really big soon and there will be demand for some brighter colours such as pinks and raspberries. Another lovely combination is chocolate brown which can look quite stunning on the right person.

"Occasionally someone will ask for soft pink or some colour that they've seen in a wedding magazine photograph.

"Invariably, though, brides do come in with one idea and go out with something completely different that suits their skin tone better.

ABOVE Gold dresses and accessories are sure to cause a flurry of excitement

"Dresses do look so different on customers rather than models. We advise customers of all different shapes and sizes. We sell anything from the slimmer straight-cut dresses to fishtails, the popular A-line and the fuller princess-type of dresses."

As with all good bridal shops, Helen takes her time to discuss exactly what the bride is looking for. "When a bride comes into Confetti and Lace we always do a consultation and try to build up a relationship with them. Sometimes they just want to buy a dress, but usually they are after the whole works, including the veil, tiara, shoes and underwear."

BELOW A veil adds a touch of sophisticated mystery

Accessorise in style

One of the essential accessories to purchase or borrow is a wedding veil. These are normally made out of lace or tulle and can be secured by a tiara.

Do have a 'trial run' at putting on the veil to avoid any last-minute panics and try to ensure that the veil will stay in place, no matter what weather is forecast for your big day. They have been known to blow off and disappear into the distance!

You may wish to have a headdress of real flowers made for the day or to choose one of the myriad of fabric floral headdresses available.

"All the headdresses made me look a bit like a female version of Julius Caesar so I went for a simple sprinkling of gysophilia through my hair," recalls Tracey. "I thought it looked great and didn't cost a fortune either."

Lingerie

This hidden layer needs to make you feel good and as glamourous as you want to be on your big day. Do try lingerie on with your dress to ensure there are no unsightly lines which will ruin your appearance.

And go for lingerie that will be extremely comfortable rather than irritating. You'll have enough on your mind.

Shoes

Comfort is again the watch-word when it comes to selecting footwear. There's no doubt that if your feet are in agony it will show on your face – not the prospect you want for your wedding day.

Do select shoes which tie in well with your outfit and remember to break them in well around the house without getting them dirty or scuffed.

It sounds obvious but if you are a particularly tall bride, you may want to choose flatter heels rather than find yourself towering above your husband-to-be.

Going away outfits

If your budget allows, you may wish to treat yourselves to something really special to wear as a going away outfit.

Do bear in mind your honeymoon destination and whether you will want to travel in the outfit. If you're being whisked straight to an airport, you'll want to be wearing something that will be comfortable during the flight, unless you can be bothered changing in the airport loo.

ABOVE Liaise with the groom to ensure you both co-ordinate

Also think about when you will actually wish to wear the outfit again. If you go for something smart and classic you are sure to set the right tone and it can come in useful for other occasions.

Bridesmaids

BELOW Not all your bridesmaids need to be in the same colour

Choosing your bridesmaids can be either simple or a minefield depending on who you have in mind and how many attendants are going to accompany you to your wedding.

After making that decision, the next choice is the colour and style of the dress. Claire said: "I had no problem choosing my bridesmaid. It had to be my sister who has been a lifelong, trusted companion and true friend.

"The only thing was I knew that she intended having her second baby around the time we were thinking of getting married.

"In the end, it all worked out fine. The baby was four months old by the time we tied the knot, so the wedding didn't clash with the birth and she even had her fabulous figure back." A pregnant bridesmaid (or matron of honour, to be strictly correct) is fine so long as you choose a suitable dress that can be altered at the last minute to suit the baby bulge.

ABOVE Choosing a white bridal dress makes you stand out from the bridesmaids with their coloured outfits

Colour co-ordination

Getting the colour right both for your wedding dress and that of the bridesmaids is imperative.

You may have some ideas in mind for bridesmaid dresses but when it comes to it, either the colours may not suit your attendants or they simply dislike them.

This is where a bridal specialist can step in to avoid any friction and (with luck!) come up with a suitable compromise. These days, bridesmaids don't all have to look identical but you may like some uniformity in their outfits or hairstyles.

Discussion is key to iron out any potential problems or financial worries. Do you expect the bridesmaids to pay for part of all of their dresses or will you foot the bill?

Several fittings before the big day are again essential. Donna reveals: "One of my bridesmaids was living miles away from me. We had one fitting months before the event and then no more until a couple of days before the wedding.

RIGHT Don't be afraid to choose bold colours for at least some of your bridesmaids

"When she came up for the final fitting she had been living a rather wild lifestyle, eating, drinking and being merry. As a result she'd put on lots of weight and couldn't fit into the dress. It was a bit of a panic but we got the dress altered. It was a headache I could have done without and I know that she squirms every time she sees the photographs as she looks rather podgy.

BELOW Matching colours helps create a co-ordinated look

Getting there

Getting to the church on time used to be such a simple exercise. The father of the bride had a friend who owned an old Jaguar. He had his arm twisted, he would clean the car inside and out, stretch some white ribbon over the vast bonnet then pick the bride up with an hour to spare and whisk her off to the ceremony. Nowadays things are different. Wedding day transportation is a multi-million pound, cutthroat business that can at first seem bewildering, when all you want to do is get there in style and comfort – and on time.

Weddings can be as simple or as complicated as you want them to be and organising the big day's transportation requirements is no exception to this. The good news is that there's plenty of choice when it comes to what you can use. You can go for something traditional like a vintage Rolls Royce or a horse-drawn carriage or, as has become increasingly popular recently, a modern stretch limousine.

The key to successful wedding day transportation, as ever, is preparation.

BELOW A classic car can add a personal touch to the proceedings

How many cars and for whom?

It's vital to address this right at the start yet so many people forget about transport arrangements until the very end of their wedding preparations. The reason it's so important is because what you decide to use, and for how many, can drastically affect your allocated budget for the day.

If you're having a small, intimate wedding, perhaps at a registry office, you might want to get a friend to drive you there but for most weddings there are a lot of people to take into consideration. Let's start with the basics:

BELOW The back of the car is where that last-minute Father to Daughter chat takes place!

There will need to be a car each for the bride (usually with her father), bridesmaid party, the bride's mother and perhaps other relatives. Decide early on whether you want to provide transportation for all of these people as many just use one car to get the bride to the ceremony, which is then used to ferry bride and groom to the reception. Whatever you decide, stick to it.

If the bride is going to arrive in an ivory-coloured Rolls Royce, it'll look strange if the bridesmaids are dropped off by a rusting Ford Sierra, so think carefully about how the cars will impact on the feel of the day. There's no need to spend silly amounts of money on wedding cars and, with a bit of thought and careful planning, you can get the cars you want at a price you're willing to pay.

Where are cars available from?

Quite simply, wherever there are people to get married, there are businesses that exist to cater for the needs of a wedding. There are many ways that you can find a suitable solution to your transport needs but the best starting point is to talk with friends and family that have already done this. You'll get an honest account of how reliable, friendly and costly it was for them, instead of listening to the sales patter of the companies that are vying for your business. You can also meet many wedding car suppliers at the various wedding fairs that are held at large hotels around the country, especially in the spring-time. They may even have their cars parked up outside so you can see them firsthand for yourself.

ABOVE An advantage of a limo is that it has plenty of room for the bride's dress

If you're still unsure, pick up a copy of Yellow Pages or any other business directory. The latest Yellow Pages, for instance, has a whole section near the back that's devoted to wedding services and the first heading is 'Arriving in Style'. Many of the advertisers have small photographs of the cars in their fleets but, for a proper look, visit their websites where there should be detailed photographs of each car available and a tariff for you to compare like with like.

Once you've short-listed your favourites, give them a call to discuss your requirements. Have your wits about you, though, and don't be forced into a corner. Remember, it's a closely fought business but there should be plenty to choose from. Some questions to ask prospective suppliers are:

- How old are the cars in the fleet?
- How often are they used and are they regularly maintained?
- Is there a guarantee of service if the car experiences a breakdown?
- How will the car be decorated?
- How will the chauffeur be dressed?
- Is there a discount available for use of more than one car on the day?
- How long will the car be available on the day?
- Is it cheaper if the car is only needed for a couple of hours or so?
- Are any extras, such as Champagne, included in the price?
- What will happen if you need to cancel or re-arrange the date?

Once you have decided on who will be transporting you and the rest of the bridal party, make a firm booking and get a written contract that details every part of the transaction. Then, at least a month before the day of the wedding, contact the company and finalise all arrangements.

BELOW What could be more romantic than a horse-drawn carriage?

A car to suit your needs

This is your big day so you'll be wanting the wedding car to be as memorable as everything else. As hinted at earlier, there are many different types of car to choose from and you might be unsure as to what's what. Rolls Royces, Bentleys and Daimlers have been the staple transportation at weddings for decades and their popularity hasn't waned at all over the years. The lure of these cars is that they are known as 'the best in the world' and therefore are quite fitting for the most important day of your life.

Some of these cars can look a little dated now, though, and a ropey old Rolls Royce Silver Shadow can be bought for as little as £5000 these days, meaning that you might end up arriving at the ceremony in a banger with clouds of grey smoke billowing behind it! Vintage Rolls Royces and Bentleys are usually a different matter but it's not just the external appearance of these cars that matters. They are silky smooth, almost silent and always luxuriously appointed. There's plenty of room in them for a bride's wedding dress not to get crumpled and, all in all, they make you feel really special.

BELOW A stretch limo will make you feel like a star for the day

A modern stretch limousine might appeal as these have become incredibly popular. Approach these with caution, though, because when they're not being used for weddings, they're often ferrying drunken young women from pup to pub. Do you really want to be taken to your wedding in a car that was cruising around the wrong end of town the night before? And, while they are fashionable at the moment, they used to be seen as naff and rather vulgar. In ten years time that image may have returned and you'll be wishing you'd used something else on your wedding day.

It's not just cars that transport brides to ceremonies. Depending on where you're getting married, it might be nice to use a traditional horse and carriage, particularly if the weather is pleasant. You'll need to be prepared to do a bit of research if that's the sort of thing you'd like and the same questions need addressing as though you were hiring a car.

Over the years, it's not just wedding ceremony venues that have become increasingly whacky and bizarre – transportation has become a little strange at times, too. Novelty vehicles such as motorised skips have been known

ABOVE If you're into cars, you may opt for something quirky, like this 2CV

to be used as transport between church and reception, while classic buses, steam rollers and even tractors have all seen active service as wedding day transport. Scooters, motorbikes and sidecars, white London taxis, boats, parachutes and helicopters have all got some appeal to somebody, but the important thing is to use a method of transport that fits in with the style of wedding that you want.

Some brides have even been known to walk to the church – and this might not be the no-brainer you instantly dismiss it as. Just think, if you live in a small, close-knit community and the ceremony is going to be held near to your home, walking could really get the day off to a tremendous start. Imagine the feeling as everyone gathers at the ends of their gardens to wish you well when you proudly walk past – you'll feel like royalty (so long as the sun is out, anyway!)

It's not just for the bride...

Let's not forget the groom, though. It's his big day too and he might fancy the idea of not being outdone by the bride when arriving at the ceremony. How many men have lusted after a Porsche, Ferrari or Lamborghini? Just the thought of being able to sit in one is enough to get most guys excited. Well, like we said, wedding day transportation is a big business and it was only a matter of time before someone came up with the idea of wedding supercars.

Just type in 'wedding supercars' when you're searching on the Internet and you'll be surprised at how many are available and almost all offer a national service – at a price, naturally. Practically any exotic car is available for this purpose if you look hard enough. Usually the hirers will go any distance asked of them and there's nothing quite like seeing all those faces drop when the groom or best man roars up outside in a blood-red Ferrari.

However the groom arrives at his wedding venue, it's a journey he'll never forget, so turning up in a supercar is a great way to make the memory a pleasant one.

Transport for the others

So you've arranged the cars for everyone involved in the actual proceedings but have you left something out? Your wedding reception and evening function are meant to be the best parties of your lives and there is bound to be plenty of wine and other refreshments flowing on the night!

As part of your arrangements it can be a good idea to lay on a couple of mini-buses or coaches to transport your guests back to their homes or

hotels so that they're not worried about who's going to drive. Taking the pressure off of everybody in this way makes it a relaxed occasion and certainly adds to the fun factor and, when you consider the costs of an average wedding, this gesture will literally be a drop in the ocean. Well worth it.

LEFT What better way for the groom to arrive in style than in a Porsche 911 Turbo?

Who's that man?

Some wedding guides pretty much ignore the groom, apart from a passing mention. Which seems odd because he's a useful part of any wedding ceremony.

All right, so there are men who are happy to sit back and let their wives (and mother-in-laws) to organise the whole shebang, turn up on the day, say "I do" and then get drunk at the reception. "I must admit, I had nothing whatsoever to do with the planning of our wedding," confesses Tim. "My fiancé and her mother sorted it all out and I just agreed to everything. It was a great day and nice and easy for me!"

Getting involved

These days, however, on the whole, blokes like to get involved in the planning of the wedding, so that it's as much 'their day' as it is the bride's. And that's the way it should be. Working as a couple means that both partners can bring their own strengths to the table and ensure that they have the wedding they want. "We had lots of fun sitting down together planning our wedding," recalls Darren. "Of course, we had the occasional argument but on the whole we got on well and it helped set the tone for life together."

BELOW Morning suits are traditional wedding garb in the UK

There are, too, some things that the groom may be better at organising. Perhaps photography, video and the cars. OK, so that's making stereotypical assumptions; some men are, of course, going to be better at arranging cakes and bridesmaid dresses; but you see the point...

Morning glory

One thing that even the most reluctant groom is going to have to sort out are outfits for himself and the other male members of the party. There are no set rules as to what the groom and his team should wear, although the traditional choice is a morning suit – typically striped trousers, black or grey tailcoat and possibly a top hat (which is usually carried, not worn).

This is simply because weddings usually used to take place in the morning (hence some people refer to the reception meal as the 'wedding breakfast') and gentlemen dressed that way at that time of day, before changing to a evening suit for, er, the evening. So, if you're being pedantic about it, you wouldn't dream of getting married in a morning suit if the proceedings were likely to go on beyond 6.00pm (or you'd disappear and change outfits for the evening).

Unless you happen to be a member of the aristocracy, though, you're unlikely to worry about this technicality and may choose to wear morning suits because they look smart, you'll all look alike and you can hire the outfits relatively cheaply. Indeed, there's little point in buying a morning suit, because you're unlikely to have many other occasions to wear one. Do make sure, though, that you book with the hire shop well in advance. "It didn't occur to me that I'd have a problem hiring a suit," confesses Andy. "However, when I marched into the shop three months before the wedding, I was told that they'd nothing available on the date we were getting married. In the end, I spent hours on the phone and finally managed to track down some suits at a shop 80 miles away. I had to drive all the way there and back to collect the suits the day before the wedding, and my dad kindly returned them the following Monday."

BELOW A dinner jacket is a smart alternative to a morning suit

Dress for dinner

Morning suits aren't to everyone's taste, though. Evening dress (a black-tie dinner suit) is a popular choice in the USA and parts of Europe, but less so in the UK, although it's certainly a smart, acceptable alternative to a morning suit. It's also an outfit you're more likely going to have use for in the future, so you may want to buy rather than hire. "I was adamant I didn't want to wear a morning suit, it's just not my thing," explained Peter. "So we agreed on dinner jackets and

ABOVE A lounge suit is ideal for less formal weddings

OPPOSITE A top hat is usually carried, not worn, unless you're very young!

everyone looked great. I've since been able to make use of the suit on the odd occasion my wife and I have been to a formal dinner."

However, morning and evening suits are not appropriate for less-formal weddings For these you'd wear what, in wedding-lingo, is called a lounge suit – essentially the sort of thing you'd wear to the office. This is a good excuse to splash out on a smart new suit (perhaps even made to measure) that you can put to good use after the event. Bear in mind, though, that you're unlikely to be able to have all the men in the party wearing the same outfit, although that's not expected at less formal occasions. And do avoid anything too high-fashion – you're going to have to live with your wedding photographs for years to come. "You should see my parents' wedding album," laughs Darren. "They got married in 1975 and my dad's wearing a white suit with a kipper tie, hanky in the breast pocket, high waist-band and massive flares. Priceless!"

Uniform approach

If you're in the military you're likely to want to wear full regimental uniform, which may limit your choice of best man. He, at the very least, needs to be dressed as you are, so he needs to be someone from your regiment. A kilt, by the way, is only an acceptable choice if you have a suitable Scottish or Irish heritage!

And that brings us to another point, Before you decide what sort of outfit you're going to opt for, talk to the other men in the wedding party before forcing them to wear something they're not comfortable with. So, that typically means liaising with your best man, ushers and the bride's father. The latter, in particular, may object to anything out of the ordinary. "My girlfriend's father is very traditional and wasn't keen on my idea of orange cravats with the morning suits," explains Mike. "We got around it by me and the best man wearing the orange ones, while the bride's father and ushers had conventional grey cravats."

As we've mentioned, the groom and best man really need to be dressed alike, for anything but very informal weddings. However, if this means regimental uniform or kilts, you may not be able to get the rest of the party matching. The solution, then is to get them to wear more conventional suits that somehow tie in with the groom and best man.

ABOVE A top hat is usually carried, not worn, unless you're very young!

ABOVE If you're in the military, you'll want to get married in uniform

Colour coding

This can be done by choosing accessories, such as ties and waistcoats, in an appropriate colour. This is an opportunity for the groom to put his stamp on the proceedings with a bright flash of colour (again, though, be sympathetic to the tastes of the other members of the party).

Speaking of colour, although it's traditional for the groom not to see his bride's dress in advance, it's useful to have some idea of the colour scheme to ensure that your bright red waistcoat doesn't clash with her lilac dress. "I fancied green bowties and waistcoats with dinner jackets," explained Pete. "However, when I came back from the outfitters and showed them to my girlfriend, she went a bit quiet. It turned out she'd gone for green accessories on her dress, but a completely different shade. She was able to give me a sample of the material and I managed to change my waistcoat and bowtie for something that tied in."

You also need to liaise on flowers. It's traditional for the men in the wedding party to all sport matching flowers in their buttonholes, and these need to tie in with the bride's bouquet and other flowers, as well as with ties or cravats.

Size matters

Whatever you go for, make sure that you're comfortable with your choice and your suit fits properly – something that's particularly important with hired outfits. "My trousers were too big on me," admits Andy. "I spent the whole day hoisting them up and I look like a school kid in an oversized uniform in the photos!"

In all the excitement of choosing a suit and tie, it's easy to forget the more mundane parts of your outfit such as shirt, shoes and, er,

underwear. Your shirt needs to be appropriate for the style of outfit and be new, crease-free and well-fitting. Shoes are usually black and do please avoid comedy socks – plain black are just fine. You can, though, wear your Mickey Mouse boxer shorts if you really want to – only one other person should be seeing those!

Going back to shoes, if you're buying new ones (and there's a far chance you will be) make sure you wear them around the house for a couple of weeks in advance to break them in. You don't want to be getting blisters on the dance floor!

LEFT It's nice if the groom's outfit co-ordinates with the bride's

Looking good

CENTRE Don't forget to pay attention to your shoes!

So, you're all kitted out in smart togs, but what about you? Are you looking your best? You and your bride are going to be focus of attention on the day, so now's the time to lose that beer-gut and clear up that greasy skin.

Nearer the time, get yourself a decent haircut, but don't go for anything too radical. "I'm going a bit thin on top, so I keep my hair closely cropped," explains Neil. "Trouble was, the night before the wedding I got out the clippers and didn't notice that they'd been changed to the shortest setting until I'd run them through my hair. I'd no choice then but to do the whole lot at the same length, and I turned up to my wedding practically bald. I wasn't popular with the missus!"

Carrying on from that, take care shaving on the morning of the wedding. You need to do a neat job, but watch out for nicks, and don't use a new aftershave in case it brings you out in a rash!

Speech therapy

The other thing that the groom has to sort out by himself is his speech. Traditionally, the groom speaks second, after the bride's father, and before the best man. Usually it's a short speech – etiquette dictates that the groom thanks the bride's father for his speech and then reel off a list of other people to thank. In other words, there's no need for him to be witty or entertaining if he doesn't want to be. Remember to

thank your new in-laws, your own parents, the guests for coming, your new wife for agreeing to marry you, and your best man for his support. Of course, you should personalise your speech with a few kind words for the people you're thanking, and perhaps present the two mothers with flowers.

BELOW The groom doesn't have to say too much during his speech

"Instead of flowers," says Pete, "I chose to give the mothers ornamental trees that would flower each May, to remind them of our wedding day. They were really touched by this and the trees now take pride of place in their gardens."

Aftercare

Finally, the groom needs to think about what to wear after the wedding. Traditionally, you'll remain in your wedding outfit for the reception, unless it's a very informal affair in which case you may want to change for the evening.

Brides tend to spend a long time mulling over what they're going to have as a 'going away' outfit. In other words, what they'll wear as they leave for the honeymoon. Thankfully, men don't have to worry quite as much, but if you turn out in scruffy jeans and trainers alongside your immaculately presented wife, you may not be popular!

So grab the opportunity to buy yourself some new casual clothes that will be appropriate for your honeymoon journey.

Photocall

Choosing the right photographer for your big day is very important. Not only do you want someone who is right for the day but also reliable enough to produce the highest quality work. Once all of the hullabaloo has died down and the honeymoon is over, your photographs are often the only material reminder of the day.

If money is tight, it can be very tempting to get a friend or relative who's a keen amateur photographer to take the pictures. The problem is that they might be able to take great photographs as a hobby, but put them in the stressful situation of a wedding and they just go to pieces.

Amateur approach

"We figured that in these days of automatic cameras we didn't need a professional," admits Laura. "Instead, we got my brother to take the photos. He's a good hobby photographer and has loads of expensive equipment. The trouble was, he'd no idea of what shots to take, and he's very shy so he couldn't organise the guests into the correct groups. He also took so long fiddling with lenses and flashguns that people got bored. He took some lovely photos of me and my husband, but we didn't get the ones of family and friends that we really wanted."

ABOVE A professional photographer will capture the true atmosphere of your wedding

Of course, some amateur photographers can produce good wedding photographs, but make sure that both you and them are confident that you're going to get good results.

The professionals

RIGHT Some photographers offer to take engagement portraits, which is a great way of building a rapport prior to the big day

For most people a professional wedding photographer is the sensible option. And the key word here is 'wedding'. There are great professional photographers who can do a superb job of shooting tins of beans, cars or fashion models, but are hopeless at a wedding service. Select a photographer who has a good reputation and the resources to provide a solution should something go wrong. Ask your friends who they used and take note of their recommendations. Is the photographer full-time and experienced? Does he (or she, of course) offer various packages and are they flexible? All these factors should be taken into consideration before booking.

Make sure you meet beforehand the photographer who is actually going to cover your wedding and view examples of their work. It is advisable to see a complete album of photos from one wedding rather than a variety of selected best images. It is important that you are confident with your photographer and can rest assured of his standard of work. You should also like him – a good photographer must be able to control the taking of the images without being bossy and dictatorial. Remember, this is a very personal day, so you don't want it spoiled by an unpleasant person behind the camera!

"My boyfriend booked our photographer over the phone and we never met him before the day," groans Beverley. "On the day this fat, sweaty man arrived. He kept calling me 'darling', which I hate, and insisted on touching the women as he positioned us. He didn't smell too good either! It put a damper on the whole day, which wasn't helped by the fact that the photos weren't anything special at the end of it."

Why skimp?

Don't be tempted to go for the cheapest person out there. Why pay £2,000 for a dress only to skimp on what is a very important part of the wedding process? Remember you are paying for expertise, experience and reputation. A professional photographer should have a complete set of back-up equipment, does not panic if it is raining cats and dogs and has the ability to rectify any problems on the day.

LEFT Your wedding is a once-in-a-lifetime event, so don't skimp on photos

Establish exactly what is included in the price. Does it include a full set of prints and an album? And on top of that what do you have to pay for extra prints for friends and family? Some photographers will charge an attractively low rate for the day, and then sting you on the reprints, often using clever sales techniques. Don't forget that most professional photographers will be VAT registered and this will have to be included in the rates.

"We chose a very pleasant photographer because he seemed good value for money," says Steve. "After we returned from honeymoon he invited us to his studio to preview the photos. We were sat down on a comfy sofa with soft music playing and the photos were projected onto a large screen. He asked us to tell him which pictures we didn't like, which was hard, so we found ourselves leaving most of them in. Next, he asked us what size prints we wanted, and when we said 10x8-inches, he zoomed down the size of the projection to that and, of course, it looked tiny, so he talked us into buying larger prints. The freely flowing wine didn't help! Over the following days he invited our parents to see the photos and order prints, and in the end he got over £1500 worth of extra business from us. Still, they are great pictures!"

ABOVE Traditional wedding groups can be given a fresh twist by making them informal

Make a list

Once you have booked your photographer, make an appointment to meet again two or three weeks before the date to go through your requirements. If you have booked 18 months in advance, it is difficult for a busy wedding photographer to remember your individual character and specific needs.

Current trends include a mix of traditional formal bridal party line-ups and contemporary, informal 'paparazzi'-type shots, resulting in a set of photographs that capture the atmosphere of the day without being too intrusive. It's a good idea to ask for some formal group shots – even if you don't want them, you can be sure that your older relatives will.

However, the worst thing you can do is to present your photographer with a long list of required photos. These can take forever to arrange and you usually find that Great Aunt Aggie has nipped off to find the loo and Uncle George has disappeared to have a smoke just when they're needed. The whole procedure starts to become long-winded and tiresome for your guests, most of whom just want to get to the reception and start imbibing. One of the most common complaints heard about wedding photographers is that they took too long and were bossy and aggressive. Traits that may be due to them having to look for missing people who should be in photos.

"Our wedding photos went on for ages," complains Nigel. "There were about 100 guests, and the photographer went through endless combinations of family groups, friends, me and my wife alone and with bridesmaids, best man and so on. I thought he was going to drag the cook out of the kitchen! By the end of it, people were getting bored and sloping off to the bar, which meant the final shot of everyone was far from complete."

It's far better to ask the photographer to go through with you his usual shoot list and then tweak that to suit your specific needs. Explain your reasoning for wanting a particular group – perhaps because your

OPPOSITE Candid reportage shots are very fashionable

BELOW It's great if the photography covers the preperations before the ceremony

parents have remarried and don't want to be stood next to each other, for instance, so he remembers to do it.

You should also establish exactly what the photographer is covering. Do you want him to start off at the bride's home, covering her and the bridesmaids getting ready and climbing into the car, and send an assistant to do the same with the groom and best man? And what about the afternoon and/or evening reception? You'll inevitably pay more for this extra coverage, so you may rather get a talented friend to take some shots both before and after the main wedding service. However, if you can afford it, having the professional cover the whole day will ensure you get consistent and high-quality results.

In advance of the date, check with the person organising the ceremony that photography is allowed during the service. Some churches, for instance, don't let you take any photographs during the vows, while others simply ask you not to use flash. Whatever, it's important that you let the photographer know what can and can't be done. When the register is actually being signed, it's usual not to take photographs, but a mock-up can be arranged straight afterwards.

OPPOSITE Try to get away from the crowds for some intimate shots

BELOW The ultimate location for wedding photos – so long as you're ready to change clothes!

Get away

Once the service is over, there's normally a rush to get off to the reception, where the group photographs are taken. However, if you can, it's a good idea for the photographer to spend time alone with the bride and groom for some romantic shots, unhindered by Uncle Jack and his old Zenith. In the USA, it's perfectly normally for the bride and groom to disappear off to a scenic location for photography while the guests congregate at the reception.

"After our wedding, our photographer whisked my husband and I off to a nearby castle," recalls Janice. "None of us had any cash to pay the entry fee but we blagged our way in past an astonished ticket collector and the resulting shots now take pride of place in our album. It was well worth doing and we got to the hotel before anyone noticed we were missing!"

OPPOSITE A good wedding picture will be good enough to frame

BELOW Wedding photography is about more than shooting the bride and groom. Shots like this are irresistable

Going digital

The digital age has opened up tremendous avenues for photography and today the majority of weddings are shot with digital equipment. It has given wedding photographers more leeway on the amount they shoot, as they no longer have the costs of film and processing. It has introduced the options to have your images printed in colour, mono, sepia or a combination of all three, without having to decide in advance which you want. Images can be greatly improved with careful on-screen cropping and offending parts or people can be removed – but remember that you'll have

RIGHT A good photographer will be on the lookout for unusual shots!

OPPOSITE You may want the photographer to cover the reception to pay for someone's skill and time to perform these tasks.

"My brother turned up at the wedding with his new girlfriend, who seemed very nice, but she ended up running off with one of my friends at the wedding," says Janice. "Obviously we didn't want her in the photos, so we got our photographer to digitally retouch the offending shots."

Don't make the mistake of thinking that now film is not involved, rates will be cheaper. Many photographers have had to invest large amounts of money in new equipment and technology to be able to offer these improved ranges of services.

Time has to be spent on the computer preparing and sorting the images. Often photographers will present the shots on disk with contact sheets – you benefit by often having a much wider choice. Don't expect a photographer to

ABOVE Digital gives you the choice of colour or black-and-white after the event

OPPOSITE Digital photography allows for some lovely special effects, such as partial tinting

supply high-resolution images on CD – the photos are his copyright and many packages are priced with the expectation of gaining extra reprint orders for relations and friends. If you do want to print your own, it may be worth asking for a quotation, but don't be surprised if this is not an option. Compare it to asking an artist to sell an original painting.

Album covers

In recent years, manufacturers of photograph albums have expanded their ranges to meet the increasing demand for a more varied range. Contemporary, reportage and minimalist styles have been introduced to complement the traditional designs. You can use different sizes to give a more interesting result and there is the facility to have a digital album where the pages are actually made with your images and bound into a book, incorporating an artistic design.

On video

While still photographs are pretty much a must at any weddings, video coverage is optional. It's entirely up to you whether or not you have a video cameraman on-hand. Some people feel uncomfortable with a video camera pointed at them while they go through the wedding vows, in which case it's best not to have the service filmed. However, you may want some informal video of you leaving the service, in which case a friend or relative could do the job. After all, so long

as you have good still photographs, it's not the end of the world if the video isn't great.

If you do opt for professional video coverage, again ask to see their credentials and samples of their work. Anyone can buy a camcorder and set themselves up as a wedding videoer, but they may not have the filming and editing skills to produce a high quality result. It can make things easier on the day if you employ the same company to do both the still and the video photography – that way you can be sure that both teams will work together.

Disposable income

ABOVE Providing disposable cameras is great fun, especially for kids

Finally, encourage wedding guests to take their own photographs. A fun way to do this is to put a disposable camera on each table at the reception. At the end of the day, get someone to collect them all up and take them away for processing. You'll end up with some fun, if not perhaps high-quality, images to augment the professional photographs.

"We asked our guests to take photos with disposable cameras," smiles Susie. "OK, so some of the shots didn't come out very well, but many were great. Some of the children at the wedding had grabbed cameras and gone off taking photos of each other and these were lovely. Also, there were some fun shots of people sitting around the table laughing after a few drinks. The only pictures we weren't too keen on were those that one of the male guests had taken of himself in the gents!"

BELOW Encourage your guests to take and share their own photos

Guest list and invitations

"Your name's not down, you're not coming in." The legendary words uttered by countless door-men and bouncers outside nightclubs up and down the country. Yes, having your name on the guest list is a big deal, whatever the occasion and wedding guest lists can, at times, be seen as the great divider. If your name's not down, there's usually something the matter.

Your friends and family will all be needed by you long after the actual day has become a distant memory, so it's important to approach making your guest list with an open mind. Excluding people who are close to you can ruin long-standing relationships and it pays to put a lot of thought into who will be asked to share in your celebrations.

Being invited to any wedding is an honour in itself – get it right as this part of the planning and preparation process will be pivotal in the success of the big day. You want your guests to feel privileged to have been able to share in your joy and to be talking about it for months (for all the right reasons). Follow these invaluable pointers and reap the rewards…

Making the list

This is one of the first things you need to do as soon as you've decided to get married. As a couple you should sit down together and compile a rough list of all the family members and friends that you feel should come. Once you've done that, if the bride's parents are footing the bill, it's the done thing to ask them who they'd like to attend.

Once you've made a list, stick to it! The reason this is so important is that the amount of people invited directly impacts on the budget that you will have allocated for the occasion. Compiling the guest list can be the cause of much heated debate for all concerned, so don't expect it to be an easy task. Once you've done it, though, the event will become more real to you and you can get on with more detailed preparations.

You might have chosen a venue already and this will dictate how many people can be invited. Alternatively you might choose the venue after compiling your guest list and go for one that can cater for the right amount of people. Whatever way you approach this, the people footing the bill should really have the final say.

Who's invited?

When putting the list together, make sure you don't forget to add yourselves! It's surprising how many problems are caused by the bride and groom not including themselves when it comes to the catering arrangements. As a matter of etiquette, you should also invite the minister (or the registrar) that conducted the service and his wife but the chances are that, unless you are on familiar terms already, the invitation will be declined.

BELOW People will be honoured to be invited to your wedding

Now, do you want to invite that boozy uncle or aunt? In any family or circle of friends there are bound to be 'characters' that are potential problems once they've had a bit too much to drink. If you feel you don't want to exclude individuals that could pose problems, the best thing to do is arrange for a mutual friend to keep a close eye on the person in question and make sure he or she doesn't go too far. Far too many wedding days have ended up as disasters because one or two people overdid it on the Champagne and caused embarrassing scenes or problems.

Obviously you'll be wanting close friends and your families with you on the day but what about their children? Here we have a potentially explosive situation because emotions can get in the way from the start so this decision needs careful consideration.

Tanya had good reason to regret attending a wedding where children were present. "From start to finish the day was a disaster. At the church I couldn't hear anything of the ceremony because babies were crying." It soon got worse, as Tanya explains, "Then, at the reception, I was barged into by a little boy and I ended up with red wine spilt down the front of my new dress – I was livid but didn't wish to cause a scene but the occasion really wasn't suitable for babies and toddlers."

But you might adore children; perhaps you've got your own already and there's no way they won't be attending. If that's the case then excluding the children of other guests probably isn't a good idea. Depending on the amount of children expected, it might be a good idea to hire an entertainer for the day to keep them all amused, enabling the parents to enjoy a bit of quality time on their own. When filling out the invitations, make it quite clear that the children are being asked along, too, mentioning them by name.

If, on the other hand, you'd like an 'adult' day without any kids around, you need to deal with this carefully so as to avoid

BELOW It's good to see a mix of generations all enjoying themselves

ABOVE It's up to you
whether or not you
invite children to
your wedding

hurt or embarrassment. The only way to address this is head on and there
are bound to be one or two upsets along the way but that's better than
having your day spoiled by unruly children.

Doting parents might not get the hint when only their names are
mentioned so the wording on the invitations should leave no room for
misinterpretation. Having 'NO CHILDREN' printed on them, though,
should be avoided. Far better to be apologetic about it, giving the
impression that this was something beyond your control, for instance:
"We regret that we cannot cater for infants or children on the day" can
be interpreted as the venue not allowing children and you really had
no choice.

However you say things on the invitations, though, it's a good idea to try and get the word out as soon as you've made your decision. Use family members to disseminate the information and be tactful when dealing with parents, particularly those that have young children that they cannot bear the thought of being away from, even for a minute. Your reasons for coming to a 'no children' decision could be down to costs, the venue or just the fact that it'll be a long day for children and there won't really be anything to keep them occupied. Be firm, though, and don't let parents push you into a corner by offering to pay the difference so they can bring the whole family. It's your day, after all.

Of course, some of the best weddings are those where children are present, because they can be the life and soul of the party – especially when it comes to the disco! They also have other uses, as Mike explains. "We took our kids to a friend's wedding and the bride's father's speech went on and on. Thankfully, I was able to make the excuse of needing to take my two-year-old son outside for a play. Out in the garden, I met some other fathers who had the same idea!"

BELOW Who said children weren't well behaved?

The wording

ABOVE LEFT
Little girls always
love a wedding!

ABOVE RIGHT A
baby always
makes for a great
photo!!

As with so many aspects of getting married, the wording on wedding invitations is usually dictated by age-old tradition. Of course, it's entirely up to you what you want to say when inviting guests to your wedding and, depending on how formal or otherwise your day will be, the invitations will need to match the rest of proceedings. There's not much point in sending out invitations that give the impression you're getting married in a cathedral when you're really reciting your vows in Elvis Presley costumes...

Usually, if the bride's family is taking care of arrangements, the invitations are sent out by them. If the parents of the bride are no longer together, though, it might be better to make the invitations from the bride and groom or name the parents individually.

However your invitations are worded, there are some essential pieces of information that always need to be included:

BELOW Weddings are a great chance for ladies to buy new hats!

- Are any extras, such as Champagne, included in the price?
- What will happen if you need to cancel or re-arrange the date?
- Names of the hosts (usually the parents of the bride).
- The bride's name and the groom's full name and title.
- Exact time and date of the wedding.
- Location of ceremony and reception.
- Which part of the day the invitation is covering.
- Whether children are invited or not.
- The time that celebrations are due to come to an end.
- RSVP address and date by which the invitations need to be returned.

BELOW Even your guests can find it all too much at times!

The wording of the invitations often follows a set pattern and whoever you are using to produce your wedding stationery should be able to advise on what is appropriate for your particular event.

These are just two examples of dozens of different types of invitation. As long as you make everything crystal clear so that there is no room for confusion on the part of your guests, this should be a straightforward affair and one that causes few, if any, problems. Just remember, that if you are having your invitations printed, to proof-read them carefully, making any necessary alterations before they are produced. Just getting the smallest piece of information wrong (such as the time) could cause chaos!

Mr & Mrs Thomas Jones
request the pleasure of your company
at the marriage of their daughter
Theresa Louise

to

Mr Philip Lloyd Wilson
on Saturday 22nd October 2005

at 11.00am
St Mary's Church, Beaumaris, Anglesey

R.S.V.P by 26th August to:
32 Green Road, London W18 8HY
0208 903 1446

Mr & Mrs Barry Robinson
request the pleasure of your company
at an evening reception to be held at
Tyndale Hall Hotel, Stroud, Gloucestershire
on Saturday 22nd October 2005
at 7.30pm
to celebrate the marriage of their daughter
Sharon Louise
with
Mr Stephen John Williams

R.S.V.P. by 26th August to:
3, Lark Rise, Leavesden, Herts
01923 540023

ABOVE a typical example of how an invitation might be worded if following tradition

LEFT If the invitation is just for an evening reception it could be worded this way

Get the timing right

Sending your invitations out a couple of weeks before the wedding day is crazy. Most people lead extremely busy lives and need to plan well in advance, no matter what the occasion. When it comes to weddings there are outfits to be planned and purchased and these things obviously take time. There are gifts to buy, too, and people love to spend quality time buying the perfect presents for the bride and groom.

But, while it's good to give your guests plenty of notice before the wedding, it wouldn't be sensible to send out your invitations a year in advance. A year is a long time and there might be unavoidable changes to plans, times, venues and so on that would render those invitations useless. Four to five months is quite sufficient for most people but your close friends and family members will be aware of the date well in advance of other people so there's no need to keep it a secret.

Day and evening invites

An easy way around the problem of having too many people on the guest list is to split things up into two halves. Perhaps you're getting married in a registry office or a church/chapel that's too small to accommodate all the guests you'd wished for. Inviting the ones that can't be fitted in at the ceremony to just the reception or evening party means there's no room for anyone to take offence.

Especially if budgets are tight, you might find it prudent to keep the numbers small at both the ceremony and reception, opening the invitations up further for just the evening 'do' where your friends can still feel a part of the big day without it costing you too much.

It is vital, though, to be totally clear about what part of the celebrations your guests are being invited to when you make out the invitations.

The wedding list

It used to be common practice for the bride-to-be to have a 'bottom drawer' which was basically a collection of gifts to help her on her way to becoming a married woman. As soon as she was in her mid-teens, friends and family would put things aside that they thought she might need, such as linen, bedding, crockery, cutlery, baby clothes and even the mother's wedding dress.

How things have changed! Marriage is often entered into by couples that have

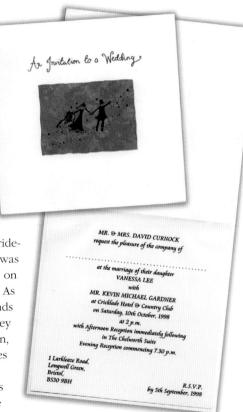

An Invitation to a Wedding

MR. & MRS. DAVID CURNOCK
request the pleasure of the company of

....

at the marriage of their daughter
VANESSA LEE
with
MR. KEVIN MICHAEL GARDNER
at Cricklade Hotel & Country Club
on Saturday, 10th October, 1998
at 2 p.m.
with Afternoon Reception immediately following
in The Chelworth Suite
Evening Reception commencing 7.30 p.m.

1 Larkleaze Road,
Longwell Green,
Bristol,
BS30 9BH

R.S.V.P.
by 5th September, 1998

ABOVE Everyone
likes a party!

OPPOSITE
A happy guest!

been living together for months or years or have lived on their own in separate homes for some time. For couples in this situation, what could the guests possibly buy them to help set them up for married life? They've probably got everything they need already.

If you've got the essentials because you've already kept a home, perhaps the wedding gift list could enable you to specify special items that you've previously been unable to afford, like silver cutlery or lovely china goods. The decision is yours but you need to take into consideration the individual circumstances of the guests that are being invited to donate these gifts.

Compiling a gift list can be tremendous fun and is a pleasant diversion from the stresses of sorting the rest of the day's activities out. Just remember that decisions made by your guests when purchasing your gifts might not be to your personal taste so try to be as explicit with your list as possible without being too pushy.

If you feel that you don't need anything in the way of household items, perhaps you'd benefit by receiving cash donations. A few years ago this would have seemed to be in extremely bad taste but etiquette is changing all the time and people now realise that newly-weds often undergo financial struggles and are more realistic about giving the couple what it is they actually need.

But what about sending the gift list out with the invitations? Again, in times gone by this would have been deemed to be inappropriate but times have moved on. It would be best to not mention the list on the actual invitation but enclosing it in the same envelope would be perfectly acceptable. If you have chosen a store to hold your wedding list (many department stores around the country offer this service) then enclose details of where the list is held.

Above all, though, the golden rule with any aspect of invitations to your wedding, is that all information should be polite, clear and understandable.

The reception

The ceremony is over and you are now a married couple – congratulations! The day has only just begun, though. There's a reception to get through yet and probably an evening of hard partying, so it'll all need to have been carefully planned to the last detail.

Planning the reception needs to be given priority as soon as you've decided on a date. It's the most expensive aspect of most weddings and whoever is footing the bill should be involved from the outset, too. Once you know where you want the reception to be held, contact the venue and make a provisional booking. Some hotels are booked 18 months in advance so be prepared to change your plans if the date has already been taken.

ABOVE If you have use of a large garden, a marquee can be an ideal reception venue

Whatever you decide upon, make sure it's something your completely happy with. With any luck, this is something you'll only be doing once, so get it right and you'll treasure the day always.

The perfect venue?

We've already looked at venues in Chapter 2 but it is nevertheless important to stress that the choice of venue is crucial when making your initial plans. Choose somewhere that will comfortably accommodate the number of guests you're inviting (or prune the guest list to suit the venue).

Make sure that they permit music and dancing and that there's a bar available, preferably for the exclusive use of your event (assuming, of course, that you want these facilities). Check out their license and ask what time your party has to come to an end. Develop a good working relationship with the management and staff, if you can, and visit periodically to make sure that everything's set for the big day.

If you've chosen to have a traditional garden party type reception with a marquee and outside catering, ensure that everything is planned well in advance and liaise with the companies providing you with the equipment and food so that there are no nasty surprises. Above all, just keep reminding yourselves that this is your big day and don't be pressured into choosing a venue that you're not really happy with. The wrong choice of venue has the potential to leave some really unpleasant memories. The right choice will allow you to relax, knowing that everything's taken care of – after all, you'll have plenty to occupy your minds!

Getting there

If your wedding ceremony is to be a civil one in a hotel then usually the reception and evening party take place there, too. If it isn't, you'll need to be quite explicit as to the exact location of the reception, particularly for guests who aren't familiar with the area.

BELOW For all but the most informal weddings, a sitting plan is essential

Enclose the address and directions with the invitations you send out. It's a good idea to also provide links to a couple of websites; one for the venue (if it has one) and one to an online map finder service such as multimap.com so that anyone can print an easily understandable set of directions.

If you've provided a mini-bus or coach service for your guests so that there aren't any drink driving worries, make sure that the time and place for collection is known by all well in advance.

Seating arrangements

Formality when it comes to where everyone is seated for the reception is becoming less prevalent but there is still a lot to consider and there's plenty of tradition to wade through when coming up with the ideal seating plan.

How and where everyone is seated might be dictated by the room used for the reception. Some couples like the idea of a big, wide top-table where the bride, groom and respective families are sat from left to right, with the other tables in two rows leading from either end of the head table at right angles. Other layouts might include several round tables spread throughout the room – it all depends on the venue, really, but having a top-table for the bridal party is widely seen as an essential part of proceedings. The rest is up to you but there are things to consider carefully when planning where everyone will sit.

BELOW The top table is where the wedding party sit, and is the hub of the reception

It's said that you can choose your friends but you can't choose your family. Family gatherings always have the potential for problems and if your parents are acrimoniously divorced or there are others with 'history' then it's best to keep these ones apart. Your friends, too, may be close to you individually but do they despise each other? You must remember who it is that you're inviting and seat accordingly. Remember Hugh Grant being seated on a table with all his ex-girlfriends in Four Weddings and a Funeral? It was an excruciating moment and very funny for the audience. Horrendous for the victim of the joke, though, so avoid little tricks like that. If seating sworn enemies near each other is unavoidable, at least warn each of them beforehand and ask them to be on their best behaviour.

BELOW The sort of food you serve may vary but a wedding cake is a must!

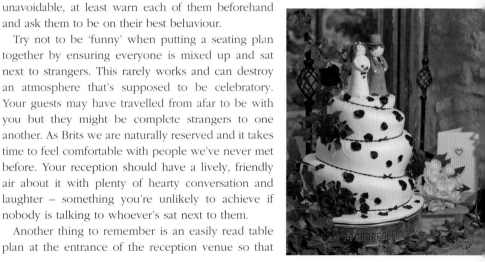

Try not to be 'funny' when putting a seating plan together by ensuring everyone is mixed up and sat next to strangers. This rarely works and can destroy an atmosphere that's supposed to be celebratory. Your guests may have travelled from afar to be with you but they might be complete strangers to one another. As Brits we are naturally reserved and it takes time to feel comfortable with people we've never met before. Your reception should have a lively, friendly air about it with plenty of hearty conversation and laughter – something you're unlikely to achieve if nobody is talking to whoever's sat next to them.

Another thing to remember is an easily read table plan at the entrance of the reception venue so that

the guests can see where they're supposed to go. With place cards already on the tables, confusion should be kept to a minimum. If there are plenty of guests to be seated, put up more than one seating plan otherwise there'll be a long queue of people waiting to see where they're seated.

Feeding the multitudes

What's your favourite food – Italian? Thai? Curry? We all have different tastes but when catering for a large group of people, you're best avoiding these kinds of cuisine (unless, of course, the guests are Italian, Thai or Indian…). There's no such thing as a perfect wedding menu, as there will always be somebody that doesn't like anything that's on offer. However a good restaurant manager or caterer will be able to sit down and discuss your requirements with you and help with some important decisions.

Consider your guest list carefully and plan a menu that will be suitable for the majority. Will there be children in attendance? If so, a large four-course dinner would be a waste so ensure they're taken care of with something suitable for small tummies. Ask your guests, via the invitation RSVPs if there are any special dietary requirements (are they vegetarian or vegan?) so these can be considered, too (indeed, it's courtesy to offer a vegetarian dish). Food allergies are no joke and people that are allergic, to nuts for example, can die if they eat the wrong thing. Not an ideal scenario for your wedding reception!

A formal, sit-down meal is the most traditional approach but if you prefer something a bit more relaxed then buffet-style catering might be just the thing for you. This does have the added advantage of enabling the guests to mingle right from the word go and it allows people to pick and choose exactly what they want to eat.

BELOW Champagne, or at least sparkling wine, is the way to greet guests

Don't be hampered by what everyone else thinks is suitable. If your wedding is an unconventional or themed event, go for whatever will fit in with the rest of the day. If it's a barbecue, a great big picnic or a pub lunch, just make sure you don't go for weird and wonderful cuisines unless you know for sure that your guests are into it too.

"I spent three whole days after John and Alicia's wedding on the toilet," owns up George, who was the best man. "They are both into really hot Indian food and that's what everyone was given at the reception! I don't mind experimenting with my food but that really wasn't the right time for it. Thankfully there weren't many guests and the children were given something else to eat. In fact, I wish I'd had the kiddies menu!"

Yes, it is your day but you don't want guests complaining that you'd ruined their day.

Drink and be merry

"I'll never forget the reception at my friend Susan's wedding," recalls Ruth. "If you saw it on a film you'd think it was complete fiction. Everybody knew that the groom was a 'bit of a lad' but nobody realised until then just how crazy he could get when he was drunk. I was a shy, fifteen-year-old bridesmaid and by late afternoon he'd attempted to grope me in some squalid cupboard, tried it on with the other bridesmaids and punched his mother in the face. Proceedings ended when he actually punched his own bride – blood was everywhere – and he was promptly arrested. He spent the following fortnight visiting every one of the guests to apologise but, unsurprisingly, the marriage didn't last long. This was twenty years ago and people are still talking about it!"

That's a fairly extreme example of what can happen when at least one of the guests (or members of the wedding party!) has too much to drink but it serves as a stark warning as to the dangers of overdoing it at a social occasion. You may be aware of some of the guests having a problem saying 'no' so perhaps it's a good idea to, instead of pretending that nothing could happen, form some sort of plan to avoid potential trouble. This may be as simple as having a word with someone level-headed that you can trust to keep an eye on mutual friends or relatives.

Alcohol and weddings have been inextricably linked for thousands of years. Even the Bible mentions Jesus turning water into wine at a wedding feast once supplies had run dry (how handy is that?). Weddings are supposed to be joyous occasions, celebrations to cherish forever so it's hardly surprising that 'dry' weddings are a rarity. But apart from keeping control of the amount of booze consumed on the day, are there any other factors to consider? Well, yes there are:

Wine and champagne

At the very least you'll need to cover the cost of a few cases of wine for the actual sit-down reception meal or 'wedding breakfast'. You may also wish to lay on a bit of 'bubbly' when the guests arrive, just to get the reception off to a swinging start and, depending on how large or small your wedding is going to be, this will have quite an impact on your budget.

Don't allow the budget to push you into buying cheap and nasty drink, though. Serving Pomagne or Lambrusco instead of champagne won't go down very well but 'New World' sparkling wines from America or Australia are often agreeable. On the tables, it's a good idea to have at least one bottle of red and one white but try to keep the wines easily drinkable. You might like your reds to be as dry as the Sahara desert or your whites heavily oaked – fair enough, but don't impose this on your guests. Go for 'medium', whatever the type of wine you choose and you won't go far wrong.

BELOW Don't forget to lay on things for the kids to do

There's no need to spend £10 on each bottle of wine, either. Consult a wine merchant and cut a deal – you should expect a discount of up to 15 percent when buying in bulk. When deciding on what wines to go for, why not take a few bottles home with you and have a fun couple of evenings trying them out? It's also best to avoid having well-known brands served (how many restaurants have you been to that serve bottles of Jacob's Creek?) because everyone will know what you've spent. Wine wholesalers and merchants supply hotels and restaurants and will be able to advise you when choosing a particular style.

Don't forget that if you're hiring professional caterers for your wedding, they'll charge you the 'going rate' for wine and you might end up paying over the odds for wine that nobody enjoys drinking, so organise this yourself – it'll be better in the long run for everybody. If the meal is to be held at a hotel or restaurant the management probably won't allow you to supply your own wine. If that's the case, sharpen those negotiating skills and get the best deal you can.

The rest of the day...

ABOVE Grown-ups, too, appreciate some distractions!

Generally speaking, unless money really is no object at all, the champagne and wine etc at the reception are provided free for guests as it's paid for by the ones organising the wedding but the rest of the day's drinks aren't.

If the venue for the evening's entertainment has a bar, that's usually sufficient for guests to keep 'refreshed' but be warned, if you offer a free bar where you cover all the drinks costs, you are opening yourselves up for a couple of possible nasty surprises. "We had no idea that people would take such advantage," says Amanda. "We offered to cover the drinks bill for the whole day and we were staggered by how much people consumed – just because it was free. Not only did some get too drunk and cause a commotion but when it came to settling up with the hotel, the booze bill was nearly £2000!"

Let's dance!

ABOVE Music is at the heart of any wedding reception

It's reasonable to assume that if you're reading this that Bill Gates isn't your uncle and neither is the Sultan of Brunei, so you won't be hiring Madonna to take care of the music. The evening function following the sit-down reception has the potential to be the greatest party of your lives and, as it's the final part of proceedings, it's the time that'll be freshest in the memory after it's all over.

Depending on the background of you and the guests, and the choice of venue, the music played can make or break the party. If you and all your friends are fanatical about classical music and the venue is a stately home, having a mobile disco or a karaoke won't be on the agenda. For most, though, the choice will be narrowed down to either

ABOVE The first dance
is traditionally led by
the bride and groom

hiring a band or a DJ. Whatever you choose, though, you need to make sure that the music played is suitable for your guests. You might enjoy headbanging to Led Zep when you're at home or freaking out to the Prodigy but it's going to be a bit extreme for poor old aunty Mavis!

"The band hired by my best friends for their evening do had simply no idea about what to play," recalls James. "It was obvious that they were big Radiohead fans because the only songs they performed were slow, depressing and hardly wedding material. It all fizzled out rather quickly – I think I lasted a couple of hours before making my excuses and heading for home."

Sound out friends and see who they recommend. If you're going for hiring a band of musicians, the general rule of thumb is that the greater the number of musicians, the more you'll be paying. If it's a DJ, check out his or her CD collection and make sure you ask for 'something for everyone'. This could include some classic '70s disco tracks, a bit of '80s and some modern, contemporary dance-floor greats. As when choosing your wine, avoid extremes in style and people won't be complaining.

It's traditional (but not compulsory) for the bride and groom to take to the dance floor before anyone else and this doesn't need to be a slushy, romantic number, but it should be something you both like. "The band at our wedding offered to do Lady in Red for the first dance," groans Pete. "I really dislike this song and refused to dance to it, so they agreed to play a Van Morrison number, which was far preferable." This is then taken as a cue for the others to join in, which is actually a good thing because people are often too shy to be the first up. If the band or DJ really know their craft, the floor will be full until the final song, leaving everyone feeling like they've had the party of their lives; the perfect end to the perfect day.

BELOW The bride and groom on the dancefloor can be a lot of fun for the guests

Countdown to the big day

O rganisation is the key to the smooth-running of your wedding. Any married couple will tell you that the event is often akin to planning some sort of military campaign.

Making a comprehensive checklist is a great way of ensuring you don't forget anything and, unless you are extremely laid-back and don't mind complete chaos, it should help to take away many of the stresses and strains involved in organising one of the biggest events of your lives.

It may sound a bit dull but if you start planning relatively early you may well avoid disappointment and frustration.

Eileen recalls: "Looking back, I really wish that Richard and I had been more organised when it came to planning our wedding.

"We hadn't a clue what we were doing and just ambled through. Eventually we set a date only to find that all the venues we fancied for the reception had been booked up months before.

"To be honest, it was all a bit of a shambles. We did get to the church on time (just) and had a lovely day but in hindsight, a bit more

planning would have definitely helped. It was an opportunity to have our dream day but we didn't get our act together and have lived to regret it. Mind you, we do have some very special memories."

Soon after you decide to get married

- If you haven't bought the ring, go ahead and choose something you will love in years to come.
- Make sure you tell all the important people, including family and friends, your special news.
- You could try to give these people some idea of when you are provisionally thinking about getting married. With any luck, you will avoid clashing with any other events that you were unaware were coming up.

- Decide whether a religious or civil ceremony will be best for you both. Choose the venue for the ceremony.
- Book the service with the vicar/priest or registrar and check how much this will cost.
- Think about asking someone to help co-ordinate the wedding if you feel you need help.
- Decide who is going to pay for the wedding and agree a budget.
- Think about how many people you would like to invite to the wedding ceremony and the reception.
- Have a look around for a reception venue and make sure it will be available on your required date.
- Start looking at holiday brochures to glean ideas for the honeymoon. Keep your budget in mind.

- Consider where you are going to spend your first night as a married couple. Do you need to book a room in a hotel or bridal suite at the reception venue or somewhere else?
- Think about taking out wedding insurance and holiday insurance to avoid anything such as the theft of wedding gifts.
- Brides can start thinking about their dress. Websites and magazines are a good way of finding out information. A file to keep cuttings in is a great idea.

At least six months before the wedding:

As the pace of organising hots up, it's time to get down to some nuts and bolts.

By this stage couples ought to have some idea about the theme of the wedding ceremony and reception.

- What sort of entertainment are you going to have at the reception. Do you need to book it?
- You need to think about bridesmaids and whether you would like a pageboy or flower girl.
- The groom needs to choose a best man and ushers.

- Decide on outfits for the male members of the wedding party, and, if necessary, make arrangements to either buy or hire.
- Book a photographer, preferably someone who has been recommended.
- Book someone to take a video if required.
- Ordering wedding stationery can take time; make sure you do this early and check it thoroughly.
- Once you have decided on the colours and theme of the wedding you can look into ordering a wedding cake.
- Book a reliable florist and agree prices for flowers.
- Will you need crèche facilities on the day?
- If you are honeymooning abroad check your passports are valid and ensure you know exactly where they are.
- If required, book a marquee.

Once the reception venue is booked you can make catering arrangements and decide on the menu and wine list. Remember that you may need to cater for vegetarians and those with special dietary requirements.

- Draft the guest list and one for the reception. Keep the budget in mind.
- Decide on the type of transport you intend to use and book it.
- Brides ought to have a good idea of the hairstyle they will want on the day and begin advising their hairdresser.

Three months before:

The next few weeks will fly by and there is a lot to do. However, try to switch off from all the planning now and again and talk about something else occasionally!

Now is the time to confirm all the major arrangements.

- Draw up your final guest list and send out the invitations with any relevant information.
- If you are having a register office wedding, have you confirmed the date?

- Decide on the music you are having at the wedding ceremony and reception. What music would you like for your first dance?
- If you are having a church service you ought to discuss the order of service with the vicar/priest.
- If you are going for a civil wedding then discuss the order of service with the registrar.
- Once the honeymoon location has been decided you need to look into visas and vaccinations. Don't leave it too late.
- Think about whether the bride wishes her name to be changed on the passport to her married name.
- Book musicians or singers for the ceremony.
- Choose a retailer if you are having a gift list and select items.
- Buy outfits and dresses for the wedding party if they are not being made.
- Ensure that all accessories have been discussed and bought.
- Establish the dates for publishing the wedding banns in both the bride's and groom's parish or else inform the appropriate register office of the intended marriage.
- Buy the wedding rings and don't lose them!
- If a toastmaster will be required, make sure one is booked.
- Brides (and grooms!) need to think about whether they would like to treat themselves to the odd pamper session and step up their health and fitness regimes.

- Confirm the accommodation for the wedding night.
- Think about organising a stag and hen night. The best man or chief bridesmaid may like to sort this out.

One month before:

Prepare yourselves for one of the busiest times of your lives. Let's face it, if you can get through the next month, it will stand you in good stead for the years to come!

Do try to stay calm. Some problems are bound to arise and even the most organised people cannot cover all eventualities.

Try to enjoy this busy but exciting time and communicate openly with your partner and anyone else who is helping you to plan.

- If you haven't already bought your shoes, lingerie and accessories, now is definitely the time. Remember to break shoes in for both the bride and groom.
- Double check bookings or the church or civil venue, the florist, photographer, video-maker, transport, hotel and entertainment.

- Plan ahead for a wedding rehearsal and ensure all the important members of the wedding party can make it.
- If you haven't already organised decorations for the reception, now is a good time. You may wish to have fresh flowers on each table and a disposable camera has become a fashionable way of each table taking pictures to be co-ordinated by the bride and groom at a later date.
- When requested, send out your gift list and when presents arrive make an efficient thank you list.
- Collect the banns certificate if you are marrying in a local parish church.
- Contact the local or national press (or both) if you would like an announcement about your forthcoming wedding to be published.
- Make sure all guests have replied and that they have details of accommodation either at the reception venue or nearby.
- Let the caterers and reception venue know about the final numbers.
- Draw up a table plan.
- Have a practice run from the bride's house to the wedding venue at approximately the same time of day the and week to avoid any hidden problems.
- Organise final fittings for bridal party.
- Agree where the attendants will get dressed on the big day.

- Check the honeymoon arrangements and order foreign currency or travellers' cheques if going abroad.
- Ask someone to collect the wedding clothes following your big day from the first-night hotel. It may need to be returned to a hire shop or stored somewhere for safe keeping.
- Arrange for any gifts brought to the reception to be stored safely until after you return from honeymoon.
- Brides try on your dress with your shoes and get a feel for how you will look on the day.
- Have a practice session with your hairdresser and make an appointment for the wedding morning.
- Brides practise wedding day make-up and try to get your skin into tip-top condition.
- Buy any extra clothes you may need for the honeymoon.

Two weeks before:

- Check that all speeches have been written.
- Hold the hen and stag nights.
- Have haircuts and bride's final practice with her hairdresser.
- Confirm any outstanding details.
- Decide whether you are going to have a receiving line and, if so, tell the reception venue.
- Contact the florist about the final numbers of buttonholes and corsages.
- Step up your beauty and health routines and try to get a little rest in between the busier times.

One week before:

- Collect foreign currency or travellers' cheques.
- Wrap gifts for the wedding party.
- Have a final fitting of the wedding dress.
- Arrange to see the decorated wedding cake and finalise how it will be brought to the reception venue.
- Advise the chief usher of the seating plan.
- Give final confirmation of numbers to the reception venue.
- Make sure the chief bridesmaid and other attendants know exactly what they will be doing on the day.

The day before:

- Ensure the best man knows precisely what he will be doing on the day and has the wedding ring.
- The groom should collect all the messages which have to be read out at the reception venue.
- Pack for the honeymoon and have the luggage taken to the first-night hotel.
- Ensure the going away outfits are at the right place.
- The bride should put out her wedding dress, accessories and jewellery.
- The groom should give any fee for the vicar/priest or registrar and organist to the best man to sort out.
- Ensure the cake is delivered to the reception venue.
- Relax and try to unwind to enjoy an early night.

The day

Have a great time and don't worry about small things going wrong –
no wedding is 100 percent perfect – and just enjoy it for the special
day it is. Good luck!

PLANNING YOUR PERFECT *Wedding*

The pictures in this book were provided courtesy of the following:

MARTIN BROWN

MALCOLM HARRIS

GREG LEDINGHAM

TUDOR PHOTOGRAPHY

PORSCHE CARS GREAT BRITAIN

JOANNA YOUNG

Book design and artwork by Nicole Saward

Published by Green Umbrella

Publishers Jules Gammond, Tim Exell and Vanessa Gardner
Series Editor Vanessa Gardner

Written by Philip and Janet Raby

Thanks to:

Kevin Hackett and Melon Promotions
for their invaluable assistance in producing this book